Robert Sowers: # The Lost Art

A Survey of one thousand years of stained glass

With an introduction by Sir Herbert Read

George Wittenborn Inc., New York 22, N.Y.

Published simultaneously
in U.S.A. by George Wittenborn Inc, 38 East 57th Street, New York, N.Y,, and
in England by Lund Humphries & Co Ltd
12 Bedford Square, London

Made and printed in Great Britain by Lund Humphries & Co Ltd

Complimentary Copy

To my wife

To Max Bernd-Cohen, first great teacher and friend

To William Johnstone

To John Baker

The best that is in these pages,
written only in their light.

Contents

page 8   Introduction

10   Prefatory Note

13   1. Origins

14   2. Traditional Technique

16   3. Medieval Stained Glass

23   4. The Triumph of Naturalism

30   5. Gothic Revival and the Craft Movement

33   6. How Stained Glass Became a 'Lost Art'

37   7. Rediscovery of Plastic Essentials

39   8. Contemporary Stained Glass

39   9. Glass Without Leads

52   10. Technical Frontiers – New and Old

60   11. Reunion of the Visual Arts

69   12. In Search of an Image

74   Notes

80   Bibliography

Introduction   by Sir Herbert Read

Mr Sowers, in the text below, gives a succinct account of the rise and fall of an art that disappeared, as a major art, with the Renaissance. We all regard stained glass as essentially a medieval art. It perished because it stepped outside the bounds of its aesthetics and tried to imitate the effects of another art, the art of panel painting, at that time pre-occupied with chiaroscuro. There is clarity in stained glass, but obscurity there cannot be without denying the *raison-d'être* of the art, which is *translucency*. The art would never have been invented had not the artists of the Romanesque period, enamoured above all by the power and mystery of precious stones, found that they could create a preciosity of great splendour by hanging panes of coloured glass between the eye and the sun. Clouds might obscure the sun, and light would wax and wane in its strength, but this gave movement and vitality to the suspended patterns. Walls that had been inanimate became frames for heavenly visions, and no art, throughout the Middle Ages, had such power and prestige with the Christian congregation.

In our own time, as part of a general return to aesthetic integrity, the art of stained glass has been reconsidered and, indeed, rediscovered. The guiding principle of translucency has been re-established, and, as in the Middle Ages, the greatest artists of our time have experimented in this medium. But there still exists a powerful opposition to this revival, which comes partly from a mistaken and reactionary interpretation of tradition (inspired to some extent by 'vested interests' – 'church furnishers' who are unable to adapt themselves to the true tradition) and partly from the modern architectural worship of bland aqueous light. The modern architect is usually afraid of colour, especially of intense colour, and rather than use it would condemn people to worship God in a white glare of antiseptic austerity. As for any use of stained glass in other than ecclesiastical buildings, the thought rarely occurs to him. Yet in every modern building there are windows through which we would rather *not* see – windows giving on to glazed courts full of soil-pipes and fire-escapes, or with larger views of gasworks and chimney-stacks. Most inhabitants of such buildings would prefer to look *at* a window by Matisse, rather than through plain glass. If the architect client cannot afford a Matisse, there are plenty of young students of this craft, as Mr Sowers shows, eager and able to demonstrate their skill.

I do not wish to suggest that the only purpose of a stained-glass window is to act as a screen for the more hideous aspects of our modern civilization. As that civilization is cleaned up and we enter into a new era of architectural beauty, stained glass will naturally take its place among the component elements of an architectural style. In the end it will be found, not that the stained-glass artist needs the support of the architect, but that the architect needs the stained-glass artist for the colour and the richness and the glory that belong to a great architecture.

This brief book attempts to define for the reader an art which, after all our far-reaching discoveries, remains something of a mystery in our midst. There is space to do little more than that. I have tried to indicate, however briefly, as many of the facets of this art as possible which link it with its past, with other arts, and with the art of the future. To do this has meant to deal with no particular period or style more than schematically. In medieval stained glass I have drawn upon English examples as much as possible, for it is my belief that English stained glass has never been sufficiently appreciated as compared to that of the continent; that in Canterbury at the end of the twelfth century and throughout England of the later middle ages were created some of the finest windows of all time. English fifteenth-century stained glass perhaps contains the most pertinent clues to the legitimate revival of the art in a key light enough to be consonant with the demands of present-day architecture.

In dealing with contemporary stained glass I have attempted to seek out those examples which, both technically and stylistically, are most in tune with the present exploratory tendencies in all of the arts. For the most part these works are very recent, many of them uncommissioned and not widely known; they are arranged visually rather than in any strict chronological sequence. It would have been better to have been able to show the work being done in a greater number of countries; however, a truly comprehensive survey of contemporary stained glass awaits more capable hands.

The text has been kept as brief as possible in order that the illustrations might have a chance to live. For that reason a section of Notes is appended to supplement parts of the text dealing with matters that may be either unfamiliar or arbitrarily stated. It is hoped that the reader will be able to ignore them initially until he has followed the visual sequence; later they may serve to lead him to the sources of many of the ideas upon which this book is based.

For the opportunity to write this book – and, indeed, to have many of the experiences which shaped it – I am indebted to the combined generosities of the Fulbright Act and the Central School of Arts and Crafts, London, whose principal Mr William Johnstone not only accorded me every facility for work during the term of my scholarship, but took me onto his teaching staff for two additional years in order that I might continue my experimentation in the school's stained-glass workshop. I cannot overemphasize my continuing gratitude to all of the many persons who helped to make possible these happy years. For what I learned of the craft of stained glass I am indebted to Messrs Francis Spear, Charles Smith, James Metcalf, and especially John Baker whose knowledge of both traditional and experimental stained-glass techniques is probably without peer; and who, moreover, helped to bring the first draft of this text to light. Mr Cecil Collins kindly read the MS. in its adolescence and offered several useful criticisms; and Mr Alfred Lammer enthusiastically devoted himself to the difficult problems of photographing *accurately* in colour some of the works included; through the kind hospitality of M. Jean Bony I was able to learn much about contemporary French stained glass and to visit the studios of his brother, M. Paul Bony, and see the designs of Matisse and Rouault which have been carried out there; Mr Stephen Bridges acquainted me with the panel of Mr John Gordon Guthrie, which the Rector of St Bartholomew's Church, Anson Phelps Stokes, Jr. kindly permitted me to photograph.

In gathering together appropriate illustrations for this work I have drawn heavily upon the resources of the Victoria & Albert Museum, the Courtauld Institute and the National Buildings Record; my thanks also to the Charles T. Branford Company, C. J. Connick Associates, Dover Publications Inc., Reinhold Publishing Corp., and Mlle Houvet of Chartres for the loan of photographs from MSS. in their possession; and to all of those other persons, artists and photographers, whose work I have tried to credit in each instance where it appears in the text. Those illustrations not so credited are in most cases my own.

Finally, my sincerest thanks to Sir Herbert Read for his introduction.

New York City, January 1954   R.S.

The Alfred Jewel
English, 9th century
cloisonné enamel.
Ashmolean.

Primitive man understood wisely when he saw a soul in all things, even sticks and stones. He responded to this soul with a deference which made him nothing if not a supreme craftsman.

Stained glass is an art of northern European peoples, who were perhaps the last such primitives in western civilization.

Their art, brought to the service of the Church, was rich in wonderment at the power of all things. About 1000 years ago their genius was brought to bear upon a number of materials and techniques in such fashion that Chartres, Bourges, and Canterbury were the everlasting result. How could one ever reawaken the energies from which these monuments were wrought? But we can take one craft, that of the glass painter, and bring our attention in close enough to focus upon his very brush stroke. We can make our own materials, the photograph and the printed page, do what they can most effectively do. They can bring together for intimate comparison works widely separated both in space and time; and windows which blaze forth in all their glory a hundred feet from the ground may be studied 'in the hand', as they were painted.

'The reason why the birth of religious painting in northern Europe – in the lands of stained-glass windows – was so belated was that for the colourist stained glass was his most powerful medium of expression. The fact that the word "painting" is linked up with pictures has paralysed us . . .'[1] Yet stained glass is certainly the most specialized of the painter's arts. It is the art most bound, as we shall see, by purely physical conditions to its own formal devices; it is an art which not only creates surfaces of imagery, but being a source of light transforms some actual place. Stained glass is thus literally an architectural element. For all of these reasons it is an art quick to die when tyrannized. How this art of stained glass evolved, flourished, and declined; how it was ignored and revived is thus a story which takes us deep into the forces which have shaped the art of the past ten centuries.

Transparent glass was invented by the Romans, and the only remains of its use in windows during the first 1000 years of our era are some fragmentary roundels found near the church of San Vitale, Ravenna. As none but the richest of early builders could have afforded to use glass, the more universal custom must have been to fill the early windows with translucent oiled paper, or horn, or with shutters and simple unglazed wooden trellis frames of the type illustrated. The lozenge pattern seen here, which resulted from the most functional

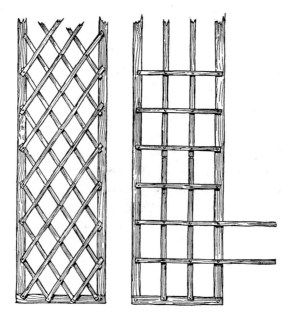

Wooden Lattice-work showing earliest form of window construction. *Drawing: J. A. Knowles.*

method of trellis construction,[2] seems to have been the source of inspiration for the leaded quarry window which later came into general use.

The art of stained glass as we know it must have been born when glaziers, inspired by the jewellers, grasped the notion of a large flexible 'lead-cloisonné' lattice-work as the way to make a window, and adapted the enamelling technique to glass painting. But such tentative beginnings lie buried in time; and with the Augsburg prophets stained glass, like the art of wall painting in the caves of Altamira, bursts into history in all of its mature glory.

2. Traditional Technique

The making of stained-glass windows has changed very little from earliest times. From the design, or cartoon (a), a cutline is made, showing the exact shapes and sizes of the pieces of glass to be cut. Colours are indicated by letters: 'R' for ruby, 'F' for flesh, etc. (b) The proper glass is selected from a stock of coloured sheets of glass and then cut to shape, a small margin of space being left all around each piece to make way for the leads. (c) The glass is then painted with an enamel which has no colour value, but serves only to render more or less opaquely the desired pattern. (d) This enamel is composed of metallic oxides and ground glass and when fired at the proper temperature in the kiln it fuses with the surface of the coloured glass. For the purpose of painting, the powdered enamel may be ground in a variety of media, such as gum arabic or oil, depending on the painting qualities desired. When the pieces of glass have been fired and cooled they are laid out in order and assembled with strips of lead. These have an 'H' cross-section and are cut to the necessary lengths, fitted around the pieces of glass (e) and soldered at all of the joints on both sides of the panel. Finally, the window is puttied to make it water-proof and it is then ready to be set into position.

All traditional stained glass has been based on these materials and techniques.[3] Since the colour is inherent in the glass, a change of colour must be effected by a change of glass and the consequent inter-mediation of a lead line. Various techniques have been developed for obtaining colour changes without lead lines. All of these techniques but one are comparatively recent and will be discussed in their appropriate place.

In the fourteenth century it was discovered how to stain glass yellow by the application of silver salts. The fact that this substance could be painted onto the glass wherever desired and fired in the same

A   B

C   D   E

The Prophet Ezekiel
French, 13th century.
(*See frontispiece and
page* 24)

Harley Roll
Scene from the Life of
St Guthlac,
English, 12th century.
This MS. consists of a long
sequence of such
roundels and is thought
to be the type of
master drawing supplied
by monastic artists for
the guidance of glass
painters.
British Museum.

manner as the traditional opaque enamel had much to do with the development of the 'gold and silver' colour scheme of the fifteenth century.

3. Medieval Stained Glass

Little is known of the earliest medieval windows. The stylistic ancestry of the Augsburg prophets, however, may be traced as far back as the eighth century, to such manuscripts as were made in the Celtic monastery of St Gall, Switzerland. With these windows begin four centuries during which stained glass was to flourish as perhaps the supreme painter's art in northern Europe.

For all that can be said of the effect of such windows, one simply has to *see* them, especially where they exist still in something like their original setting; at once cold and fiery – luminous as if themselves the source of light – incandescent, icy prisms, mapping the cosmology of an ideal.

St Gall Codex 51, St Luke, *c.* A.D. 750. *Stiftsbibliothek, St Gall.*

18

Augsburg
The Prophets
Daniel and Joseph,
11th century.
F. X. Zettler, Munich.

Chartres
Madonna and Child.
12th century.
Et. Houvet,

Canterbury   Methusaleh, *c.* A.D. 1200.
Victoria and Albert Museum. Crown Copyright.

Gloucester   St Peter, 14th century. *National Buildings Record.*

Almondbury, Yorks   Virgin and St Anne, 15th century. While the appearance of this window is somewhat marred by the close proximity of the protective screening behind it, the latter enables us to realize the lightness and *transparency* of the stained glass of this period. *F. H. Crossley*.

Winchester College Chapel
SS. John the Evangelist and James the Less and the Prophet Zephaniah, *c.* A.D. 1400.
Now in the Victoria and Albert Museum.
Alfred Lammer.

Medieval art evolved from archaic hieraticism toward naturalism, paralleling unconsciously in some respects the development of Greek art some 1800 years earlier. But while Greek (and Greco-Roman) art was allowed by history its full cycle of growth, medieval art was interrupted midway by a Rome-inspired revival of that earlier art in a much advanced state of naturalistic refinement.

In the thirteenth century, stained glass had been part of a living cosmology of materials – the arched openings in massive stonework, subdivided geometrically by means of iron armatures into orders of medallions and quatrefoils; into each of which had been fitted a panel of glass, its coloured fragments threaded with a nerve system of imagery and bound together by a lattice-work of lead – each material thus serving the whole in an order as if conceived by Plato, had the philosopher been an architect of matter rather than of man.[5] To an art whose materials were so delicately adjusted the new aesthetic could bring only disorder, that ingenious lie whereby it became intriguing to make one kind of matter seem to *be* another.

It may have begun in the painting of ornamentation, this new 'art of make-believe'. In the Romanesque churches wall painters had recalled the legendary glories of ancient marble halls with all manner of formal fantasies, witty fresco commentaries on that noble stone, the audacious zig-zags and stripes and painted panellings that one can still see in the old churches of Poitou. But 200 years later, next to the fourteenth-century Giottos in Florence, there came to be painted on

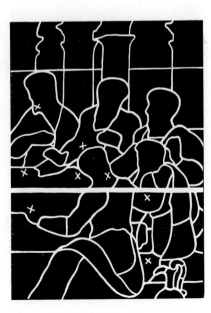

Lattice-work Diagrams
Ezekiel and
The Last Supper,
(*see pages* 24–25),
showing in the former
how the necessary
structure of leads is
utilized to create a
formal pattern in which
the subject matter can
exist; in the latter the
chaotic *formlessness*
which results (especially
at the points indicated)
when leads are
considered nothing more
than an unfortunate
necessity. The figure at
the left inadvertently
acquires a goatee, almost
loses his left hand
(on the table), etc.

24

The Prophet Ezekiel
French, 13th century.
Victoria and Albert Museum.
Crown Copyright.

The Last Supper
French, 16th century.
Detail.
Victoria and Albert Museum.
Crown Copyright.

the walls *trompe l'œil*, fake marble panels as a cheap substitute for the 'real thing'. And gradually, in the centuries that followed, the image of man too was to become *fake human* . . .

'Neither in Greek nor in Gothic art is there any pose', Oscar Wilde was later to observe. 'Posing was invented by bad portrait painters, and the first person who posed was a stockbroker, and he has gone on ever since.'[6]

By the sixteenth century it was not unusual for the glass painter to be given the task of imitating in stained glass a 'school of Raphael' fresco cartoon. Engraved reproductions of such works, by Marcantonio Raimondi and others, at the time were being circulated throughout Europe, and these were being accepted by the newly ascending mercantile patron as the final word in taste. Fine Art had been born and was beginning to be 'applied' to certain of the traditional arts. In

Chartres
St John the Baptist,
13th century.
Et. Houvet.

this new hierarchy easel painting had become supreme and all of the other arts were practically shamed into imitating its effects.[7] With his own standards of excellence thus revoked, the stained-glass artist, like the tapestry maker, illuminator, and mosaicist, was reduced to a common labourer, his traditional skills committed to the four winds. He was held to a formula alien not only to his instincts, but to the very nature of his medium. He could neither liberate himself from the structurally necessary network of leads nor could he any longer, in his effort to imitate the characteristics of painting, allow them to retain their normal decorative function. He had to try to *hide* them. Thus the 'lost art' of stained glass was never really lost; it was thrown away.

Chartres
Detail from a Grisaille
Window of the
14th century.
Et. Houvet.

The civilization of the Middle Ages was, in time, to fail as had all those countless civilizations before it. But medieval art, fanatical, lyrical, intimate in turn, though ever-increasingly naturalistic, never lost its essential harmony with nature, always conceded to each material and each craft the right to identify itself in the proper performance of its function. Riotous fantasy there was, but never the lie. It is the expression of an age that we now think of as mystical and 'unworldly'; while to that succeeding age which was to indulge in every manner of pose and artifice we attribute a 'revival of learning'.

When art is working it heightens both the materiality and the fantasy of the image; the two are fused in exaltation. But when the

The Virgin
English, 15th century.
Fragment.
Victoria and Albert Museum.
Crown Copyright.

material is excited to no purpose, or the image rooted in no material there can be no deep-rooted art. Whenever the art image has evolved to a stage where it resembles the retinal image the two have usually become confused and the latter has become the criterion of the former. The objective of the artist thus fully predetermined makes impossible such sympathetic communion between man and material as alone can give birth to the work of art. The metaphor is lost, the material flogged, and in the end even Michelangelo is superseded by Madame Tussaud's wax museum.[8]

By the eighteenth century, stained glass, like painting and sculpture, was largely committed to a corpulent, patternless naturalism

Chartres
Detail from the
Vendome Chapel,
15th century.
Et. Houvet.

sponsored by the taste of the courts and academies. Only in those arts humble enough to be overlooked by the cultural arbiters of the day had people been able to continue an artistic tradition that was more than fashion deep.

5. Gothic Revival and the Craft Movement

Neolithic rhythms of the North and the imagery of the Mediterranean East nourished Christian art for the 1000 years that ended with

Sir Thomas Burnett by William Peckitt of York, 18th century. A Royal Academy portrait on glass — unfortunately cracked across the middle. *Victoria and Albert Museum. Crown Copyright.*

Doll English, 18th century. *Victoria and Albert Museum. Crown Copyright.*
English Traditional Slipware Dish by Thomas Toft, 18th century. *Victoria and Albert Museum. Crown Copyright.*

Cimabue. The burden of inspiration then shifted to the vision of individual genius, to Giotto, Massachio, Piero della Francesca. The first great revival centred around the Laocoon, unearthed in the time of Michelangelo. Academies were born and art acquired a Hellenistic façade.

In the 300 years that followed, indigenous tradition died a lingering death. The great figures of the period, Rembrandt, Blake, Goya, Daumier – whose roots struck so much deeper than the fashions of the day – were no longer municipal idols so much as rebels and eccentrics.

The Gothic revival of the nineteenth century was a belated effort to check this tide of cultural attrition. In the teeth of an industrial age Ruskin could only look backward, Morris towards a new craft movement. Theirs was but the first unsuccessful attempt to find an ethic for modern man, 'the maker of things by art' – doomed because it could not come to terms with the machine.[9]

how galahad sought the sangreal and found it because his heart was single so he followed it to sarras the city of the spirit

Sir Galahad Following the Holy Grail   Workshop of William Morris, from a Cartoon by Sir Edward Burne-Jones, *c.* 1885. *Victoria and Albert Museum. Crown Copyright.*

American Art Glass
c. 1900
*From C. J. Connick's
'Adventures in Light
and Colour.'*

But some of the stained glass which came out of William Morris's workshop shows a sense of material, and above all a sincerity, which transcends both Victorian sentimentality and the commercial stained glass that is still predominant in our own day.

6. How Stained Glass Became a 'Lost Art'

Different processes, different conditions, different branches of art . . . In an opaque painting the radiation of the colours is absolutely under the control of the painter, who . . . can diminish or augment it at will. The radiation of transparent colours in glass cannot be thus modified by the artist whose whole talent consists in profiting by it to work out a harmonic scheme on a single plane, like a rug . . .

Viollet-le-Duc's essay, 'Vitrail', was written about a century ago during the first great movement to preserve the monuments of medieval art, and it is still the most thorough and painstaking analysis of the medium of stained glass that has ever been written.[10] Faced with the task of restoring the ancient glass of the French cathedrals, his craftsmen had in fact to rediscover the art of the medieval glass painters beyond all scholarly speculation. Their work led Viollet-le-Duc to conclusions whose implications are still not generally appreciated.

Our most able workers . . . have completed ancient windows with such a perfection of imitation that one cannot distinguish the restorations from the old parts. They have in this way gained ample knowledge of the processes not only of the material workmanship, but of art as applied to this species of painting.

This craft of the stained-glass worker cannot then be a mystery or a lost art.

What have been lost or forgotten during many centuries are the true methods which are alone suitable to painting glass; manners dictated by the study of the effect of light and optics; manners perfectly understood and employed by the glass painters of the twelfth and thirteenth centuries, neglected from the fifteenth century on, and afterwards disdained, in spite, as we have said, of the immutable laws imposed by light and optics.

In such passages may be found deep rumblings which foreshadowed our age of discontent, during which the great figures would seek by any means, jibes, mockery, ridicule – even a cult of ugliness – to break down a heritage which seemed to have smothered the senses. We are still in that age; and the remarkable thing about Viollet-le-Duc was his dawning awareness of these issues at a time when Cézanne was still a bank clerk. 'Vitrail' is the work of an enlightened Minister of Public Monuments, monuments which included Bourges and Chartres; so the drawing-room concern with form as propriety was put aside. In its place came the questions: 'What did this art do?', and 'What made it work?' One answer was found in stained glass: that its materials were arranged in such a way as to reveal their natural beauty – an arrangement which is not arbitrary but evident in the physical properties of the medium, in its 'immutable laws'. Such laws in the end *define* the medium:

> . . . the artists who composed the windows of the twelfth and thirteenth centuries showed their absolute submission to these laws, and turned them to their own ends with as much intelligence as modesty.[11]

There had been a living tradition, the power of which we can scarcely comprehend, binding every particle of this art into its place, focusing it into symbols fully resolved, at once decorative and hieratic.

Radiation Properties of Coloured Light
Given a constant shape (C), white has a piercing quality, blue a very luminous and expansive quality; while red tends to contract, and yellow remains relatively stable when seen at a distance.
From 'Vitrail'.

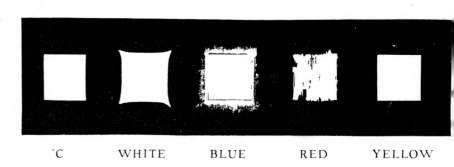

C   WHITE   BLUE   RED   YELLOW

The following excerpts from *Vitrail* show how even such decorative devices as beaded borders and the highly conventionalized linear treatment of drapery in the early windows were conceived to exploit the effects of the expanding and contracting radiational properties of different colours. This is one of the most dynamic properties of coloured light, especially when it is seen at a distance:

... let us imagine a design in glass worked out according to Fig.2. The black lines indicate the leads (see A). The compartments R are red, the compartments L are blue, and the bands C white. Here is the effect that will be produced at a distance of about twenty metres (see B).

The circular blue compartments 'l' radiate as far as the dotted circles, and the red remains pure only in the middle of each compartment 'r'. The result is that all the surfaces 'o' are red tinged with blue, that is violet; that the dividing whites between the tones, not having any coloured radiation of their own, are lightly tinged with blue in 'v' as are also the leads themselves; that the general effect of this glass is cold and purplish over the greater part of its surface, with spots 'r' harsh if you are close to the glass, sombre if you are at a great distance away from it. Now if (see A) we diminish the field of the blue discs by black painting, as is shown in D, we neutralize partially the radiating effect of these discs. If instead of white bands C we place yellowish or greenish white bands, and if we draw lines on these bands as is shown at 'e' or beads, as at 'f', then we obtain a much better effect. The blues, being heavily surrounded by black designs and further picked out with black internally, lose their radiating faculty. The reds are then much less tinged with violet by their proximity. The yellowish or greenish tones of the filets gain in delicacy by the blue tones which, tinting each of their ends, leave between a warm part which ties with the reds, especially if we have taken the pains to increase the value of the leads by the beading or by simple internal lines.

... painting applied on glass should, even in the most heavily shaded parts, allow the natural tone to be seen not through a film, but in bits of pure colour; because a shadow which completely covers a coloured glass gives, at a distance, an opaque tone that does not partake of the real colour of the glass, but rather of that of the neighbouring colours in accordance with their radiating properties. Thus to

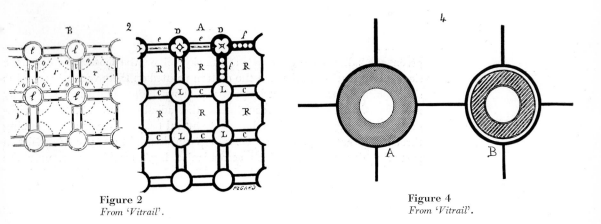

Figure 2
From 'Vitrail'.

Figure 4
From 'Vitrail'.

Figure 5 *From 'Vitrail'.*

make our explanation clear, consider (Fig.4) a disc of red glass 'A' surrounded by blue glass; if we place around this disc a shadow (even though it be itself translucent, like a slightly opaque film), this shadow will partake not of the natural red tone of the glass, but of the blue radiation of that surrounding. From a distance it will assume a false and dull tone, a mixture of brown and blue, which will make the surrounding blue seem hollow, lacking in solidity, and the red tone glaring. If, on the other hand (see B), we have taken the pains to paint this shadow on the disc not flatly, but by hatching, and at the same time leave a pure red rim all around, this rim and the interstices left between the hatchings will give the shadow a natural red tone and the blue will preserve its own quality. The rim and the interstices of the hatching will assume sufficient value, owing to the opposition of the black lines, to combat the radiation of the blue tone and leave to the shadow on the disc its natural red colour.[12] Let us examine the application of this formula. Here (Fig.5) is a fragment of the beautiful window of the cathedral of Chartres, which represents a 'tree of Jesse'. This window dates from the middle of the twelfth century. The background is blue . . . The king's robe is of wine colour, warm purple, the mantle emerald green, the pallium and the crown are smoky yellow, the shoes and cuffs of the sleeves red. It will be seen that the pattern painted on these vestments consists simply of a succession of hatchings which allow the ground colour, especially near the edges, to show between, so that the radiation of the blue of the background is neutralized by these bursts of natural tone of the vestments shining through the hatching. These observations which might seem to contradict in part the demonstration which accompanies Fig.2 are, however, only the corollary thereto. In Fig.2, we saw that to neutralize the effect of the radiation of the blue tones over the red tones, we diminished the surface of the former by opaque painting, a sort of openwork screen with contours deeply cut in patterns.

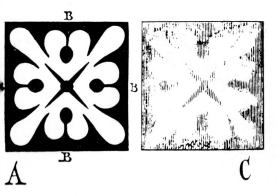

Figure 6
From 'Vitrail'.

Now, at a distance, if the transparent colour under consideration is powerfully radiant, this quality is greatly diminished by the use of the pierced screen, but, on the other hand, this same property of radiation causes the pierced screen to appear diffused, the interstices of pure colour merely losing somewhat of their relative colouring value. The contrary effect is produced with colours of feeble radiation; their colouring intensity is increased by reason of the small amount of the surface which is left pure between the lines of the screen. For example (Fig.6) assume a piece of blue glass A, whose radiating surface has been diminished by the opaque or screen B. At a distance this blue glass will produce the effect indicated at C. The further away one goes, the more indistinct the painting will become, but at the same time the blue will tend that much toward the grey. If a piece of red glass be painted in the same manner, the further away one goes, the more the painted screen will encroach on the clear glass, at the same time losing little of its opaque quality, until at a great distance the red can only be distinguished by sharp touches, as indicated at E, but these touches gain in colour intensity what they lose in extent.

The more reason one sees in Viollet-le-Duc's analyses, of which the above are but a fragment, the more incredibly retrograde must seem the renaissance view towards stained glass – and indeed toward many of the arts – an arrogance accompanied by ignorance of sheer technical essentials. But it is not hard to imagine how unacceptable, if not incomprehensible, such a view must have seemed until almost the present day. This fact, coupled with the recent neglect of stained glass, has made it far simpler to keep on thinking of stained glass as a 'lost art'.

Different processes, different conditions, different branches of art . . .

7. Rediscovery of Plastic Essentials

Art finally exploded out of the academies where it had been all but stifled by the proprieties of official taste. To the revolt artists brought not only their frustrations, but highly specialized interests which had

St Bartholomew's Church, New York   Haghia Sophia, by John Gordon Guthrie, c. 1930.

De Still Composition   by Theo Van Doesburg, c. 1920. *Le Verre*.

Compositions of
Glass Fragments
by Josef Albers,
Bauhaus, 1921.
Charles T. Branford Co.

become normal in our analytical age. Cézanne was followed by a host of 'ists' – pointillists, cubists, futurists, suprematists, constructivists, dadaists, surrealists, expressionists, vorticists, purists – who proceeded to rediscover and develop important, but often limited, aspects of art which had been largely ignored for 500 years.

Out of all these diverse efforts, however, has been reborn the common conviction: 'that plastic art never derives from a special way of seeing the world, but from a way of making it'.[13]

8. Contemporary Stained Glass

Beginning with this conviction the contemporary stained-glass artist returns to the origins of his art in the lattice-work. He asks the first question first: What do these materials do? Then he collaborates with their possibilities to forge his image.

9. Glass Without Leads

The limits of the art that is called to mind by the term 'stained glass' must be considered arbitrary,[15] since we have seen what a relatively small part 'staining', literally, has played in it. The substitution of other metals, stone, or concrete for the traditional leads – or their use in combination – offers many possible avenues of exploration for the painter, sculptor, and architect.

Along with the autonomy of the arts we may begin to rediscover the true sense of their practical interrelations.

The Convalescence by Joep Nicolas, Amsterdam, *c.* 1925. *Le Verre.*

Opposite page: **The Acrobat** by Roland Ginzel, London, 1951. *Alfred Lammer.*

Opposite page
Harlequins
by Edward Veevers,
London, 1951.

Right
The Lady in Red
by Terry Obermayr,
London, 1953. Detail.

Centre
**The Destruction of
Little Gidding**
by Kieth New,
London, 1951.
Royal College of Art.

Below
Composition
by Geoffrey Clarke,
London, 1951.
Royal College of Art.

Composition   by Adolph Gottlieb, New York, 1953. *Borgenicht Gallery.*

The Apple Eater by Robert Sowers, London, 1953.

46

Assy
The Passion of Christ,
executed by Paul Bony
from a painting by
Rouault, 1947.
Rouault's manner of
painting, in part inspired
by medieval stained
glass, returns to that
medium in a familiar
manner.[14]

47

**Broadcasting House,
Cologne**
Five-story window in the
staircase,
by Georg Meistermann
1952. Detail.
Johanna Schmitz-Fabri.

Schweinfurt
St Kilian's Church,
Window by
Georg Meistermann.
Hans Heer.

48

Vence
Chapel of the Rosary
designed by Matisse,
1947–50.
Windows were executed
by Paul Bony, Paris.
Lucien Hervé.

Panel for a Private Chapel Switzerland by Evie Hone, Dublin.

Johannes Kappelle von Eurikon, Zurich Sea, Switzerland, window designed by Max Hunziker.

Glass and Stucco Panel   Arabian, 17th–18th century. *Victoria and Albert Museum. Crown Copyright.*

Apartment Building, Marseilles   by Corbusier, completed 1953.
Exterior and interior view of glass and concrete colour screen in the foyer. *Jane Fiske Mitarachi.*

Glass and Concrete
Window
by Jean Barillet,
Paris, *c.* 1950.
Jean Barillet.

10. Technical Frontiers – New and Old

The contemporary artist who comes to stained glass will find a number of glass-working techniques, such as aciding, embossing, plating, and staining,[16] which used singly or in combination can produce effects of colour and light hitherto undreamed of. Except for staining, most of these techniques were developed after the decline of medieval stained glass, and thus have seldom been used except in the interest of a very insipid 'naturalism'.

The panel illustrated combines the effects of aciding, plating, and staining to get an infinite number of possible transparent colour changes within a single leaded area (see detail opposite). Pieces of blue 'flash' glass, which is actually a thin skin of blue glass laminated onto a basic white sheet glass, were 'stopped out' and portions of the blue flash eaten away with hydrofluoric acid in a manner similar to that used by etchers to bite a copper plate. Red flash was treated in the same manner, and finally yellow stain and the ordinary opaque glass paint were applied where desired and fired onto the glass. By plating, which consists of simply superimposing two or more separate layers of glass within a leaded area, all of the spectral colour combinations became possible.

In the modern kiln it is possible to fuse a mosaic of coloured bits of glass onto a transparent plate glass ground, as may be seen in the work of Dom Norris and Peter Ostuni (pages 54 and 59).

Even the traditional materials continue to reveal new and un-expected possibilities, however. Glass paint ground in a suitable medium becomes applicable with a pen instead of a brush. The lift ground technique, used variously in the making of batik, the dyeing

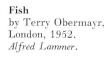

Fish
by Terry Obermayr,
London, 1952.
Alfred Lammer.

Detail of Fish nearly actual size, showing
the range of colours that can be achieved within
any given leaded area by means of aciding, plating,
staining, and painting. *Alfred Lammer.*

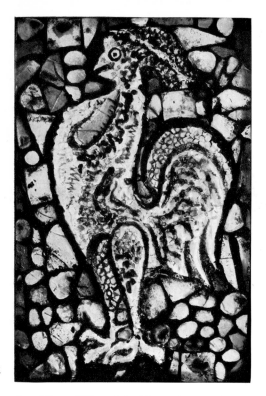

Coq d'Or and **Blessed Cuthbert**   by Dom Charles Norris, O.S.B., Buckfast Abbey.

of Easter eggs in Slavic Europe, and by contemporary printmakers, can also be applied to glass, both to aciding and painting. And in considering all the different methods of manipulating glass paint and stain, such as scratchwork, painting on both surfaces of the glass, etc., one soon leaves behind the realm of effects which cannot be carried over from canvas to enter that which could only exist in coloured glass.

In the end not mere innovations, but a greater sense of the qualities of *transparency*, *translucency*, and *opacity* are what will further this art; qualities which we may realize again are at least as aesthetically real as the bishop's nose. From them – along with all of the properties which were studied by Viollet-le-Duc and Charles Winston – can evolve once more the means of the glass painter. As an artist he will play with surfaces of light, letting it flood through in sharp particles here and there, staining it in places, or toning it with thin films of paint that create translucent, neutral surfaces here, or he will dam the light completely with areas of opaque painting there. Throughout the whole he will at the same time weave structurally the armature of leads, now embedding them in areas of opacity, now finding them again and having them march boldly counter to the painted form, defining it. But this is only to continue to rediscover as Winston and

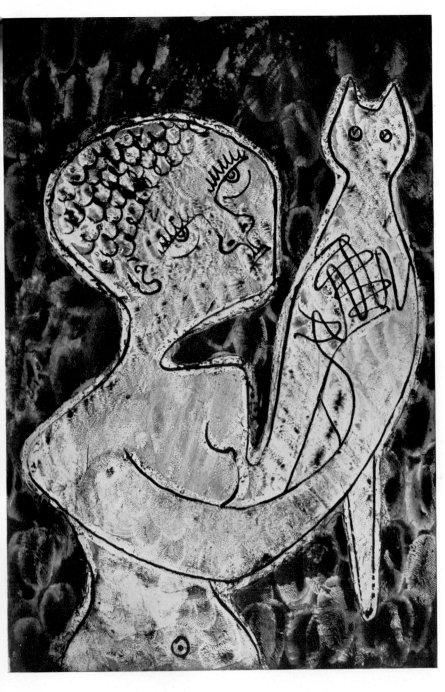

Figure with Cat
by John Baker, London
1952. Experimental
techniques, including
the 'lift ground', were
employed. Approximately
two-thirds actual size.
Alfred Lammer.

Viollet-le-Duc were rediscovering 100 years ago devices that were
mastered by the glass painters of 800 years ago – and in so doing to
liberate stained glass finally from the servile imitation of their
incidentals.

That stained glass remains what it always was, a means of modify-
ing the natural daylight of an interior, is due to a healthy prejudice

56

**Church of St Theresa
Montmagny**
by Auguste Perret, 1925.
*Libraire Nationale d'Art et
d'Histoire.*

Audincourt
windows designed by
Fernand Léger and
executed by Jean Barillet,
Paris, 1950–2. Detail.
Lucien Hervé.

in favour of its greatest effect. Only secondarily may it be considered as a kind of painting or colossal jewellery, related as it is to both.

In the nuances of certain light ratios lie the means for successful or unsuccessful collaboration between stained-glass artist and architect. Simple as they may be in themselves these ratios have not been operatively understood since the Middle Ages.

First, only so long as *more light comes through stained glass from the outside than falls on its surface from inside the room* can we see through the glass and thus see its colours and patterns illuminated.

Second, the darker the glass the *less light can come through it;* therefore the less light it can tolerate on its inside surface without losing its luminosity.

Third, not too much more light must be allowed to come through a stained-glass window than the eye is normally accustomed to *in the given interior* or the effect is harsh and glaring.

Thus the logic of medieval windows in their settings: deep, rich colours in the earliest churches where windows are few and far between and the interiors thus naturally dark; and lighter, more delicate harmonies in the late Gothic windows where the whole wall is opened up to admit light.

(Hence, it may be hoped, we will become aware of the barbarous effect when stained glass is seen in a light box. Not only is its function as a window caricatured, but all of the enlivening effects due to the qualities of transparency – the full, shimmering play of light and

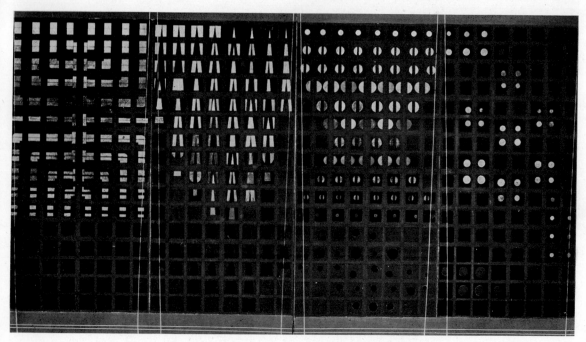

Baccarat 'Luminous wall' for the Church, designed by a team of artists, Claude Idoux, Albert Lenormand, Denise Chesnay, and Paul Reynard, and under construction. Detail of the maquette. *Denise Chesnay.*

shade on the irregularities of the glass, the action of forms dimly sensed beyond the glass which, as one moves more correspondingly — are lost, and in its stead one gets a flat, gaudy effect not unlike the front of a juke box. If this device is to remain as a necessary expedient for exhibition purposes it should cease to be such an innocent one, especially in the case of permanent museum installations. However, the effect of light boxes on early windows is somewhat less brutal than on recent work due to the eroded surfaces of most ancient glass.)

Stained Glass 'Collage' by John Baker, from experimental texture fragments executed by students and instructors of the stained-glass workshop, Central School of Arts and Crafts, London, 1952.

Composition   by Peter Ostuni, New York, 1953. *Borgenicht Gallery.*

Head of Christ   French, 11th century. Fragment showing the designed use of transparent, translucent and opaque areas.

Detail of stained-glass panel   showing the flattening effect of artificial, diffused lighting in the lower portion.

The concept of architecture as the common meeting place of the arts
has been almost lost or, more accurately, rejected after a period when
even fifth-century basilicas were garnished with cupids and cornu-
copias.[17] For the past 100 years architects have been fully engaged in
recovering their own identity. Yet, a parallel struggle has taken place
in the other arts, and one wonders – where will the arts meet again to
reinforce one another as they have done in the great epochs of the
past? As Gyorgy Kepes says, 'Architecture and painting do not meet
each other today because both are incomplete'.[18] In order to estimate
the present situation we must remember what has happened to these
arts in the past century, however briefly.[19]

In architecture, the principal materials and techniques of the
machine age – the steel frame, reinforced concrete, and large surfaces
of glass – had already indicated their unprecedented possibilities by
the turn of the century. In both Europe and America the first great
modern buildings had been built, largely by engineers and a handful
of architects of unusual insight. In their works – the Crystal Palace of
the Great Exhibition of 1851, the Hall of Machinery of the Paris
Exhibition of 1889, and the office buildings of the 'Chicago school'
during the same period come to mind – there is little or no ornamentation. Utterly frank and unassuming, such works simply embodied new
forms, achieved new economies of space and materials, and placed
these at the disposal of their users. Almost after the fact it was
discovered that these buildings were beautiful. But the great promise of
such pioneer works was followed by a half-century of confusion,

Tile Facade   Church of St Francis, Pampuhla, Brazil, by Candido Portinari, 1942. Oscar Niemeyer, architect
From Stamo Papadaki's 'The Work of Oscar Niemeyer' Reinhold.

Canterbury
Vault of the Apse
c.1180.
Walter Scott.

whose many facets all had one common denominator: 'art conscious-
ness'. On the one hand there was sentiment rampant, and the
cultural inferiority complex of the *nouveau riche;* in America, Louis
Sullivan was stopped at the height of his career by a plague of reaction,
during which skyscrapers grew like weeds and were fitted out with all
the trappings of San Marco. Meanwhile, on the continent there
evolved an extremely doctrinaire modernism; an equally ostentatious
lack of ornamentation; the negation of colour and texture – a period
when buildings, even domestic, were made to aspire to the condition

of grain elevators. Such were the currents that shaped, with only a few notable exceptions, the main body of architecture up to the 1930's. The intimations of art as a normal social process had been almost too much for both factions; and, needless to say, neither was in a position to offer any significant opportunities to the image maker in any of the media that had formerly complemented great buildings. But the past two decades have brought us, in spite of war, to a new phase which promises to be of more positive significance.

The architects have begun to solve the problem of ornamentation – at least on monumental buildings – on their own terms. The main body of a building now becomes defined as a 'slab', which can then be perforated, notched, raised on stilts, glazed, and textured by its own necessary surface components: casements, sills, glass, etc., and set off effectively against its appended substructures. This solution seems fully appropriate to the techniques of the industrial age; the once barren forms of twentieth-century buildings become enriched, but by surfaces which no longer vainly seek to evoke the handiwork of an army of ancient craftsmen.

And what of painting? Here we must go back further. When painting emerged as a fine art it was freed from its traditional walls and texts.[20] Because of its plastic amenities oil painting became the art most able to satisfy the demands of an increasingly individualistic form of patronage. When that patronage grew too vulgar in its demands artists of integrity had, like Rembrandt, to become both father and mother to their best work. In time taste became a profession and gentlemen of refinement undertook to establish once and for all the canons of beauty. 'God forbid that truth should be confined to mathematical demonstration!', cried Blake, largely in vain. Only a ripening of this condition was needed to reduce creative integrity to a private matter and to make the cliché every man's meat.

First naturalism, then a whole swarm of 'isms' have come to pick at the substance of art.

Oil painting *as a medium* was largely realized by the time of Rembrandt; and the more or less profound succession of fashions which have followed since his day show that the artist, in spite of himself, has not been unaffected by the attention span of his limited, and now economically waning audience of the salon. An art once freed is now an art dispossessed.[21]

It will be seen that most of the revolutionary developments in the plastic arts of the last hundred years have still taken place within the pattern of the production of *objets d'art* for the delectation of the connoisseur. Only in its most recent phase does painting begin to point beyond such limits in its very *intentions*. It may be convenient, momentarily, to look upon contemporary art as the product of three generations which, for our purpose, may be seen essentially and supra-individually as the bearers of three seminal ideas.[22]

The earliest can be called the generation of prime-movers; of artists who, like Picasso, Matisse, and Klee, were born at the time and with the genius which enabled them to revitalize Western art with some of its primitive energy. What can be said of their art? These great figures have earned and received an indelible recognition; but have also with justice been accused of 'drinking from the common cup and producing private little streams'; of plundering the past. Yet, does this not begin to emerge in perspective as the role set for their generation? We have reviewed how under the impetus of Leonardo Da Vinci easel painting had imposed, by means of an academic snobbism, its own decorum on all the other plastic arts, causing them to lose their own traditional identities: tempera, fresco, mosaic, tapestry, sculpture, and, as we have seen, stained glass. But having finally wrung all the novelty out of its own resources painting proceeded to destroy its own identity by harkening back to these other arts for *petites sensations*. Picasso's *Young Girl at the Mirror*, for example, though it is an exceptional painting by current standards, makes allusions to stained glass which seem false and contrived in the presence of a fragment from Chartres. Picasso commands here neither the scale nor the conviction of the traditional artisan whose image bespeaks the accumulated wisdom of untold generations.[23] Neither can he evoke like the Coptic weaver the sense that his fantasy *emanates* from his object. So much is manipulated; so little finally revealed. Thus the nostalgic side of this great innovator is seen – possibly the last residue of that renaissance aim which we, with André Malraux, have called the 'art of make-believe'. However that may be, such art remains within the consciously personal tradition of easel painting as the creation of *objets d'art*.

Next came the generation of prototype-makers, of whom Van Doesburg, Ozenfant, and Moholy-Nagy could be called typical. Their painting is closely related to the doctrinaire phase of modern architecture; and just as the architects of that period created the 'machine for living', these painters used easel painting as a platform from which to proclaim the beauty of mechanical forms. Their work has had a beneficial effect on the design of industrial products, but the vocabulary of forms which they brought to painting did little justice to the range of discourse that can take place between hand, brush, paint, and vision. The work of the prototype-makers might as well have remained

Chartres Signature of Window given by the Water Carriers, 13th century. Detail. *Et. Houvet.*

Girl Before a Mirror
oil painting by
Picasso, 1932.
*Museum of Modern Art,
New York.*

on the drafting boards to which its most seminal ideas have returned but for the value of relating itself to the general movement of modern art. When seriously confused with the human art of image-making, as in the case of Oscar Schlemmer for example, it can only evoke the *Weltanschauung* of 'Modern Times'.[24] Yet this limited art, in its tendency toward the suprapersonal, may perhaps be another link in the chain – who can say for certain? – which, however obliquely, moves us toward some communal idiom of the future . . .

Finally, we face the present generation, which may come to be known as the generation of calligraphers, and which is contemporary with the architecture of the 'slab'. If we look once more at that

Coptic Textile   9th century. Fragment, approximately actual size. *Victoria and Albert Museum. Crown Copyright.*

architecture's ornamentation, we will see that it is achieved by the juxtaposition and repetition of relatively few discreet forms within a module or grid. In a large building this solution is ideal. It remains empirical, in that the architect is able to design his units, window casements, etc., to suit that *particular* building and still have them mass-produced. Moreover, the impersonal precision of such units seems absolutely appropriate to the monumental façade and multi-sectioned interior. Yet, are we not here at the limits of such machine art? Does not our modern industry, which produces in large quantities so cheaply and in small quantities so dearly, condemn all builders on a lesser scale to the use of *preconceived* standardized elements to achieve what rhythm and grace they may? Are we not then in fact bound by the aesthetic of the prototype-makers? It is against this spectacle – which extends throughout the whole range of things that were formerly made individually by human skill to meet the occasion – that the generation of calligraphers is arrayed.[25] These painters reassert the final claim of the human element in art; the *sense* of the contact between surface and medium; the empirical cultivation of an artifact during the process of its making; the kinaesthetic performance which in the *act* of painting involves not merely the eye and the mind, but the whole state of being of the artist in a manner analogous to that of the violinist or athlete. The most dramatic statement of this point of view is to be found in the work of Jackson Pollock, who has gone so far as to eliminate the traditional contact of brush with canvas to empha-size the human measure of the viscosity of the medium, the very gesture of drawing form. The painting of the abstract expressionists is too highly charged to remain within the frame of the easel painting; certainly it is no longer related to the space above the mantelpiece. One sees painters like Pollock working on a tremendous scale as if to embrace a whole wall. Need one doubt that this 'abstract expression-ism' is, quite literally, pure *painting*? Its calligraphic affinities with Islamic and Oriental art are far from superficial.[26] Yet its very purity reveals the dilemma: the epithet, 'space cadet', thrown at such pain-ters in the United States reaches home to the poverty of imagery that extends across the world of art like a great drought. The never-never land between the decorative and the symbolic has now become the battlefield on which the artist must cry for a *place*, literally, in our environment – where art can gain that meaning which it only has when celebrating vital human activities.

One wonders how all of these intentions can be brought together under a common roof without a common ideal. In the catacombs there was an image without art; are we now to have an art without image?

3, 1951 oil painting,
by Jackson Pollock,
New York.

**Ceiling for an
Engineer's Drafting
Office**
by Eduardo Paolozzi,
London, 1952.
Hand-printed wallpaper,
retouched *in situ*.
Nigel Henderson.

The Mass-produced Facade
Park Avenue, New York, 1953. This building was completely surfaced with aluminium panels in six and a half working days.

12. In Search of an Image

We are beginning to remember that the identity of an art can only be found in its limitations, its poetry in the imagination, and its function in society.

Under the present state of affairs only a small fraction of the population is able to earn a living by the exercise of its sensibilities, the majority being committed to the semi-stupor of some kind of drudgery. The 'hard-headed realist' is content with this state of affairs; his god is Production and it is thriving – with white bread, pre-sliced, in sanitary wrappers and *Quo Vadis* for the masses. But even this uneasy equilibrium, which at least occupies man's time, is threatened by technological developments that no one has the power to halt. According to Norbert Wiener, who is one of the leading scientists responsible for its development, the electronic computing machine has brought us to the threshold of a second industrial revolution. The time is at hand when every routine aspect of the production line can be mechanized:

> . . . the machine plays no favourites as between overall labour and white-collar labour. Thus the possible fields into which the new industrial revolution is likely to penetrate are very extensive and include all labour performing judgements of a low level, in much the same way as the displaced labour of the earlier industrial revolution included every aspect of human power.

Only where work is varied or organized on a small scale will this development be impractical or uneconomical. And it is imminent:

> We are already as far along in the process of developing a unified system of automatic control machines as we were in the development of radar in 1939. Just as the emergency of the Battle of Britain made it necessary to attack the radar problem in a massive manner, and to hurry up the natural development of the field by what may have been decades, so too, the needs of labour replacement are likely to act on us in a similar way in case of another war.
>
> Under these circumstances, the period of about two years which it took for radar to get onto the battlefield with a high degree of effectiveness is scarcely likely to be exceeded by the period of evolution of the automatic factory.

Dr Wiener's conclusions are axiomatic:

> . . . the automatic machine is the precise economic equivalent of slave labour. Any labour which competes with slave labour must accept the economic conditions of slave labour.
>
> Thus the new industrial revolution is a two-edged sword. It may be used for the benefit of humanity.

But above all, this scientist pleads, let us not forget that

> When human atoms are knit into an organization in which they are used, not in their full right as responsible human beings, but as cogs and levers and rods, it matters little that their raw material is flesh and blood. *What is used as an element in a machine is an element in the machine.*

The italics are Dr Wiener's.[27]

The machine can liberate us from a measure of servitude, but it is up to us to achieve the status of human dignity for ourselves. It is only art that makes man fully human, for only art exercises all of his sensibilities. We are talking about a concept of art here that the anthropologist is more likely to understand than any 'art lover'. Art, not in the sense of self-expression or even connoisseurship (though these have their place), but in the traditional sense of a vocation or calling.[28] Consider even the art of painting in this vein in the Far East, where its tradition has been the most durable of all. The young hand, in learning to hold the chopsticks with which to eat, thus learns to hold the brush with which he will write; and writing is but a further preparation for his ultimate alphabet.[29] In the end, the Japanese artist is the master of eighteen different brush-strokes for the rendition of drapery alone; he comes to know the bamboo leaf 'in the wind', the bamboo leaf 'heavy with rain'; the face of the four seasons – all in brush-strokes so direct and transparent in execution as to admit of no uncertainty. The man must be literally in tune with his universe, for the 'spirit of the brush' is attained only in a genuine communion between body and image, a performance that the Easterner considers to be truly religious and the living measure of a painter's worth. And in traditional subject matter the artist finds, not limitation, but common ground for discourse[30] with the artists of all previous ages upon the ultimate realities that can be measured by the senses of mankind.

In all traditional societies it was assumed that proper vocational training produced the artisan who was then valuable to that society for what he could produce by *his art*. Whatever other restrictions may exist, to the extent that there is a dispersion of the knowledge of means and ends there is a *democracy of techniques*. This cannot be denied: that the greatest security any man has ever had lay in the indispensability of his skills; while his greatest satisfaction has come from using them in the creation of what have seemed to him unquestionable goods – if that term may still be employed in its original sense. It is only by such means that any society thus far has assured that each profession necessary for the provision of its needs could have its irrevocable measure of dignity.[31]

In seeking the deepest meaning of our art in the great traditional sense of the term we have had to venture far beyond the limits of its own techniques. Our story of stained glass has led us to no final conclusions about the future of that art. We have seen its happy age when, throughout the provinces of Europe glass painting had, like Eastern art, that measure of eternal certainty. We have followed its

From the Eighteen Laws for the Lines of the Dress
'The Suppression' lines; 'The Chasing Clouds and Running Water' lines; and 'The Broken Reed' lines.
From Henry P. Bowie's 'On the Laws of Japanese Painting'. Dover.

Fladbury, Worcs.   Madonna and Child, 14th century. *National Buildings Record.*

evolution as far as we could, and then have spoken more generally of forces which now seem to be in play – and which in the long run seem likely to determine the fate of all of the forms of art. Perhaps we have been able thereby to give further meaning to key questions: What does the maker do to his material? What does the act of making do to the maker? And, what does a society want of what is thus made?

Notes

1. ANDRÉ MALRAUX. *Psychology of Art*, Vol.I, page 37. Pantheon (New York 1949).

2. 'The diamond shape of the openings between the laths is the result, not of considerations of taste, as might well be imagined, but of motives of economy and practical necessity. It is obvious that it is much more economical to fill a frame for a narrow window by placing the laths diagonally across from side to side rather than straight across, as by this method the whole length of the laths can be used and there is no waste except at the corners, moreover, the laths can be nailed to the frame at both ends, and so are stronger, whereas, if they are placed parallel to the sides of the frame . . . it is necessary to join two laths together in order to reach from the top to the bottom of the window, with the consequent loss of strength.' J. A. KNOWLES. Leaded Lights and Ornamental Glazing. *Jour. of the Br. Soc. of Master Glass Painters*, Vol.VII, No.3, page 136.

3. For a more detailed description of the various processes, tools used, etc, *see* J. A. F. DIVINE and G. BLATCHFORD. *Stained Glass Craft*. Frederick Warne & Co. (London 1940); *also* CHRISTOPHER WHALL. *Stained Glass Work*. John Hogg (London 1905).

4. cf. DOM CHARLES NORRIS. Stained Glass. An Introduction to its History and Appreciation. Parts II and III. *Jour. of the Br. Soc. of Master Glass Painters*, Vol.VII, Nos.2 and 3, for a concise and intelligent discussion of the colour aspirations of the medieval glass painters.

5. cf. ERWIN PANOFSKY. *Gothic Architecture and Scholasticism*, pages 30–8. The Archabbey Press (Latrobe, Penna 1951), for a discussion of the scholastic principle of *manifestatio*; i.e. the perfect articulation of the parts of the whole and the parts of parts. (See drawings opposite.)

6. *The Epigrams of Oscar Wilde*, page 63. Redman (London 1952). On another occasion this most perceptive of moralists in disguise observed that, 'In a very ugly and sensible age, the arts borrow, not from life but from each other.' ibid. page 58.

7. To get the flavour of this unprecedented attitude it is necessary only to recall Leonardo's famous harangue against sculpture as a Fine Art. Sculpture, he says, is a *mechanical* art, for 'the sculptor in creating his work does so by the strength of his arm by which he consumes the marble, or other obdurate material in which his subject is enclosed: and this is done by most mechanical exercises, often accompanied by great sweat which mixes with the marble dust and forms a kind of mud daubed all over his face. The marble dust flours him all over so that he looks like a baker; his back is covered with a snowstorm of chips, and his house is made filthy by the flakes and dust of stone. The exact reverse is true of the painter (taking the best painters and sculptors as standards of comparison); for the painter sits before his work, perfectly at ease and well dressed, and moves a very light brush dipped in delicate colour; and he adorns himself with whatever clothes he pleases. His house is clean and filled with charming pictures, and he is often accompanied by music or by the reading of various and beautiful works which, since they are not mixed with the sound of the hammer or other noises, are heard with the greatest of pleasure.' As quoted by SIR KENNETH CLARK. *Leonardo Da Vinci*, page 82. (Cambridge 1952).

Articulation of the 'Parts within the Parts'
Chartres, elevation of the Nave, c. 1195, and Canterbury, armature of a stained-glass window, c. 1180.

This image, of the serene, godlike dispenser of art, is still enthusiastically maintained by those who, consciously or unconsciously, despise or distrust the effects of a flourishing popular art.

8. 'As for Michelangelo, who knows what we might have been spared had he disappeared on the completion of the Sistine Chapel ceiling? True, we should be without the fascinating nightmares of the Medici tombs; but how many distorted, heaving, bulging, monstrosities we should have been spared, not so much of his own as of his fellows, whether architects, sculptors, or painters down to our own day almost!' BERNARD BERENSON. *Of Rumor and Reflection*, page 246. Simon & Schuster (New York 1952).

9. For an interesting analysis of this movement and its failings *see* SIR HERBERT READ's *Art and Industry*, Part I. Faber (London 1934).

10. 'Vitrail' was written for Viollet-le-Duc's monumental encyclopaedia of French art, *Dictionaire Raisonné* (1853–1869). Eugène Viollet-le-Duc was born in 1814 and died in 1879. For sources of English translations of 'Vitrail', *see* bibliography.

11. This revaluation of the medieval attitude is also echoed by one of the most significant philosophers of the period. Charles Pierce, who in 1871 wrote: 'Think of the spirit in which Duns Scotus must have worked, who wrote his thirteen volumes in folio, in a style as condensed as the most condensed parts of Aristotle, before the age of thirty-four. Nothing is more striking . . . than the complete absence of self-conceit on the part of [the medieval] artist of philosopher. That anything of value can be added to his . . . work by its having the smack of individuality about it is what he has never conceived . . . whatever originality emerges is of that inborn kind which so saturates a man that he cannot himself perceive it.' As quoted by W. B. GALLIE. *Pierce and Pragmatism*, page 58. Pelican (London 1952).

12. cf. *also*, CHARLES WINSTON. *Hints on Glass Painting*, pages 247–9. John Henry Parker (Oxford 1847), for the concise and accurate formula that stained glass 'will be dull, if its lights be not kept clear and bright, whether its shadows be strong or weak; opaque if its shadows be not transparent, notwithstanding the brilliancy of its lights, and heavy if the aggregate volume of the shadows greatly exceeds that of the lights'. Winston continues: 'A coat of enamel brown smeared smoothly and evenly on the glass will exclude the light more completely in this state than after it has been rendered irregular in its texture by the process of stippling. For this process collects the colour into little lumps or dots, leaving interstices between them less loaded with colour, and consequently more pervious to the rays of light than any part of the ground before it was stippled. A stippled shadow is therefore always more transparent than a smear shadow of equal depth.' This principle, probably the most important single principle in glass painting, is still so little understood that 100 years after Winston one hears of 'modern' windows being painted 'smooth' with an air-brush – proving again how ignorance, too, can be mechanized.

13. ANDRÉ MALRAUX, op. cit., Vol.I, page 156.

14. Rouault, whenever he has departed from his true medium, easel painting, to make tapestries, ceramics, or even engravings – has conceded very little to that other art form. Rather, he has been content to hire the best French craftsmen to torture their material into pseudo-'Rouault's', complete with all of the accidental, or at least purely *painterly* effects of his brushwork. If this essay shows anything, it shows the consequences of such dilettantism in the past. Hence the curious paradox that while the Rouault windows are more deeply spiritual in *content*, the lighter windows of Matisse at Vence, by comparison almost frivolous, penetrate more deeply into that mystique which it is the peculiar province of stained glass to evoke. Whatever this may be attributed to – perhaps Matisse's recent experience with coloured paper cut-outs, similar to stained glass in the fact that one starts with given flat colour areas with definite contours, has been contributory – the windows at Vence are undeniably closer to the early windows when judged in terms, not of the qualities to which they allude, but rather those that they *embody*.

15. It might be just as well to concede to the popular meaning of this imprecise term: 'the leaded church window'. A term without any such parochial connotations, for example 'colour-window', could easily be adopted for contemporary secular windows and for all of those windows incorporating obviously new materials and/or techniques.

16. Coloured enamels are unsatisfactory; technically, because of their tendency to flake away, and aesthetically, because they lack the brilliancy of colour and the *transparency* of actual glass.

17. '. . . painting, at the end of the Middle Ages, tends to encroach upon, to re-direct, and finally to triumph over all of the other arts.' '. . . each one of the arts is attempting to live for itself and to liberate itself, until the day comes when it may take its own turn as the dominant art.' HENRI FOCILLON. *The Life of Forms*, page 10. Wittenborn (New York 1948). cf. *also* A. C. SEWTER. *Painting and Architecture in Renaissance and Modern Times*. Tiranti (London 1952).

18. GYORGY KEPES, in an address, 'Visual Form-Structural Form', Los Angeles, December 1949; *Arts & Architecture*, (March 1950), page 49.

19. To make more than a few remarks here would be to go beyond the scope of the present work; the standard reference is S. GIEDION. *Space, Time and Architecture*. Harvard University (Cambridge 1941).

20. Art, in being freed from the Church did not become *free*: 'Only now and then when the feeling of relative security prevails, will art relax and pretend to have no practical aims, to be there for its own sake, for the sake of mere beauty and pleasure. But even then it will retain certain social functions, being still the expression of wealth and power, a form of conspicuous expenditure and leisure. And this will not be all. Art will serve the interests of the ruling classes by merely describing and, implicitly justifying their outlook on life, their moral standards, their scale of intellectual values.' ARNOLD HAUSER. The New Outlook. *Art News*, (New York, Summer 1952), page 45.

21. This is not to suggest, as Sir Herbert Read makes clear, 'that no great works of art were produced in the epoch of cabinet painting. From Giorgione to Picasso a host of exquisite creations . . . were produced for the capitalist market, for the private delectation of merchant princes and rampageous tyrants, for men of taste who also happened to be men of wealth. But the whole basis of that kind of pro-duction has gone. . . . tyrants have been tamed and the man of taste impover-ished . . . Only in America does private patronage survive on a considerable scale.' SIR HERBERT READ. The Fate of Modern Painting. *The Philosophy of Modern Art*. (London, Faber & Faber 1952), pages 65–6.

And in America? In 1944, a poll of the 500 *most frequently exhibited* artists showed that on the average and after an average of twenty years of professional work these artists were able to earn less than $100 a month from their art. cf. ELIZABETH MCCAUSLAND. Why Can't America Afford Art? *Magazine of Art*, (January 1946).

'O dear Mother outline, of knowledge most sage,
What's the First Part of Painting?' she said: 'Patronage.'
'And what is the second?' to please & Engage,
She frown'd like a Fury & said: 'Patronage'.
'And what is the Third?' she put off Old Age,
And smil'd like a Syren & said: 'Patronage'.
WILLIAM BLAKE, from *To Venetian Artists*, 1808–11.

22. It must be emphasized that the following schema is no more than a concise, if arbitrary, attempt to give some order to the developments which seem to be leading painting away from the *easel* painting. For anything more than this the reader should consult the standard reference works on twentieth-century art.

23. 'Modern pictures are, no doubt, delightful to look at. At least some of them are. But they are quite impossible to live with; they are too clever, too assertive,

too intellectual. Their meaning is too obvious, and their method too clearly defined. One exhausts what they have to say in a very short time and then they become as tedious as one's relations.' OSCAR WILDE, op. cit., page 53.

24. A most revealing comparison can be made between the robot visions of Oscar Schlemmer and such satirical works as the *Twittering Machine* of his Bauhaus Colleague, Paul Klee, in the collection of the Museum of Modern Art.

25. This movement is centred in post-war New York and is thus too recent and still too much in a process of evolution to be more than tentatively appraised. cf. MORSE PECKHAM. The Triumph of Romanticism; and WILLIAM SEITZ. Spirit, Time and Abstract Expressionism. *Magazine of Art*, (Washington, November 1952 and February 1953, respectively).

26. The sense of the unfaltering, directly executed, and thus predominantly linear gesture of painting is also one of the most universal traits of folk art (i.e. fractur drawings and ceramic painting – and, in our own debased, commercialized form, comic strips). It is also the method *par excellence* of medieval glass painting. Such deceptively simple looking figures as those in our illustrations can only be imitated with the greatest of difficulty – as anyone knows who has attempted this. They are the product of a very highly developed calligraphy: 'Whatever be their linear patterns, popular arts seek to preserve that expression of the past which is threatened by the forms of civilization, whence aristocratic art arises – an expression of that uncharted sea of time across which civilizations like lost armadas glide to oblivion.' ANDRE MALRAUX, op. cit., Vol.III; page 61.

27. NORBERT WIENER. *The Human Use of Human Beings*, pages 212–13. Houghton Mifflin (Boston 1950).

28. 'In a vocational order it is assumed that every trade (i.e. "walk" of life) is appropriate to someone, and consonant with human dignity; and this means in the final analysis, that if there are any occupations that are *not* consistent with human dignity, or any things intrinsically worthless, such occupations and manufactures must be abandoned by a society that has in view the dignity of all its members. This is, then, the problem of the use and abuse of machines: use if the instrument enables the workman to make well what is needed and in the making of which he can delight, or abuse if the instrument, in which some other party has a vested interest opposed to the workman's own, itself controls the kind and quality of his product. The distinction is that of the tool (however complicated) that helps the man to make, from the machine (however simple) that must be served by the man whom it, in fact, controls.' ANANDA COOMARASWAMY. East and West. *Am I My Brother's Keeper?* John Day (New York 1949), page 83. (Published in London as *The Bugbear of Literacy*, by Dennis Dobson.)

29. cf. HENRY P. BOWIE. *On the Laws of Japanese Painting*. Dover (New York 1952) (first published, Elder, San Francisco, 1911); especially Chapter II.

30. 'During those periods when importance was attached exclusively to the subject because it was inseparable from the appearance and spirit of the social edifice, no one spoke of it, no one thought of it. In periods when men say it has no importance they speak of nothing else.

'The "subject", like money, is only a means of exchange . . . But it is this role, precisely, that gives the subject its importance and confers upon it perhaps a hierarchical existence which the schools have abased to the point of folly . . .' ELIE FAURE. The Spirit of the Forms. *History of Art*, Vol.V. Harper (New York 1930), pages 330 and 333.

The enthroned Madonna and Child of the twelfth century, the still life bottles and guitars of the cubists – and, for that matter the sonata form and the 'blues' – are, however we choose in our folly to rank them, forms of communion which call forth the artist in the man: '. . . simple significant forms to follow, and to compose suddenly, by an imaginative flash, into great creations, *that are still continuous with the familiar principles they transcend*'. SUSANNE K. LANGER. *Feeling and Form*, page 53. Scribners (New York 1953); (my italics). The artist without a subject is like one who has been trying to stretch a rubber band and can find nothing strong enough to hold the other end of it.

31. '. . . since even quite common men have souls, no increase in material wealth will compensate them for arrangements which insult their self-respect and impair their freedom . . . unless industry is to be paralysed by recurrent revolts on the part of outraged human nature, it must satisfy criteria which are not purely economic.' R. H. TAWNEY. *Religion and the Rise of Capitalism*, 3rd Mentor ed., page 233. (New York 1952).

'To the worker who cannot receive technical gratifications from his work, its market value is all there is to it. The only significant occupational movement in the United States, the trade unions, have the pure and simple ideology of alienated work: more and more money for less and less work . . . The sharp focus upon money is part and parcel of the lack of intrinsic meaning that work has come to have.' C. WRIGHT MILLS. *White Collar*, page 230. Oxford University Press (New York 1951).

Bibliography of Selected Works on Stained Glass

AUBERT, MARCEL. *Stained Glass of the 12th and 13th Centuries from French Cathedrals*. Iris Books. Batsford (London 1947). (New York, Oxford University Press.)

Journal of the British Society of Master Glass Painters, London.

CONNICK, C. J. *Adventures in Light and Colour*. Random House (New York 1937).

LEE, LAURENCE. Modern Secular Stained Glass. *Architectural Design*, Vol.XXI, No.5 (London May 1951).

RACKHAM, BERNARD. *A Guide to the Collections of Stained Glass*. Victoria & Albert Museum (London 1936).

READ, HERBERT. *English Stained Glass*. G. P. Putnams (London 1926).

Bulletin of the Stained Glass Association of America, San Francisco.

STETTLER, MICHAEL. *Swiss Stained Glass of the 14th Century*. Iris Books. Batsford (London 1949). (New York, Oxford University Press.)

VIOLLET-LE-DUC, EUGENE. 'Vitrail', translated by Leicester B. Holland, from *Dictionnaire Raisonné de l'Architecture Française*; published serially in *Stained Glass*, Vols.XXVI-XXVII, 1931–2; also in part, in the *Jour. of the Br. Soc. of Master Glass Painters*, beginning in Vol.VII, 1937. 'Vitrail' has also been privately printed by Francis P. Smith, 1135 Lullwater Road, Atlanta, Georgia.

WINSTON, CHARLES., *Hints on Glass Painting*. J. H. Parker (Oxford 1847). (Contains translation of portions of the *Diversarum Artium Schedula* dealing with stained glass, written by the eleventh-century monk, Theophilus.)

ZCHOKKE, FIDTJOF. *Medieval Stained Glass of Switzerland*. Falcon (London 1947).